*diary of a tree*
Goli Khalatbary

MAGE PUBLISHERS
WASHINGTON, DC
2006

*book one*

to:   *my parents for the roots*
      *India for the land*
      *each and everyone of my friends*
      *for the tree*
      *and to you for the light years*

                              *Goli Khalatbary*
                              *Delhi*
                              *Autumn 1993*

*today a leaf left me*
*to meet autumn*

*I'll have to laugh with the nightingale*
*as the wind picks up*

*my friend    the crow    visited me*
*bringing news from the city*

*sorry I'm late    it said*
*I had to cross the desert*

*I dreamt of a god wearing earrings of rain
were they someone's tears or just memories?*

*fingers playing on moonstrings
I sketched the dawn on night petals*

*the painter sat under my branches*
*drawing the horizon with great precision*
*straight lines are so unintelligible*

*scarecrow remarked*
*they always express themselves like that*
*scarecrow understands artists*
*I understand lovers*

*this evening the lovers were*
*discussing time    forever    they said*

*one had eyes full of golden fields*
*the other   the voice of a shepherd's flute*

*the air smells of smoke and
unspoken farewells*

*my friend the crow wears black
scarecrow wears colours (some)
I wear greetings to the rain*

*as I stand here yearning for something
as essential as breath
the fog lifts*

*by noon it will be clear*

*I stand alone*

*notes:*
*heard the wolf     heard the owl*
*heard something receding*

*migration is over     accept it*

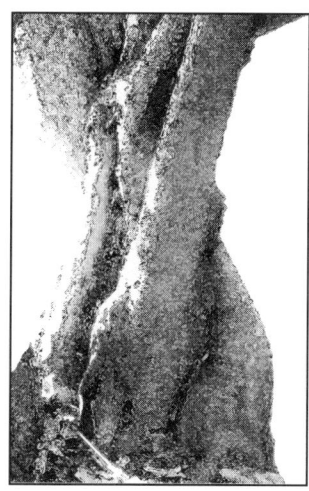

*…….been brooding……….*

*storm thunder lightning*
*the skies are angry*
*the child hugged me*
*whispering protect my sanctuary*
*I said quickly to cover up*
*the bitterness do not disclose*
*you have such a place*

*I remember crisp mornings
birds chattering     hope a wild flutter
eager to fulfill its awakening*

*the chatter continues*

*the traveler:   long ago*
*when I was homesick*
*you told me to study the spider's web*

*…images of elaborate confinement…*

*don't threaten me on the hinges
of silence     scarecrow*

*on windless days the grass
confines its birth in me*

*you only hear the wings of flight*

*and now that familiar fear is
clutching me again    what if some
forgotten prehistoric animal gnaws
my roots away? I'll be floating
in a nothing embrace*

*hold me within your sigh    my world*

*I feel so old     something is reshaping the landscape with blind annihilation*

*I feel so old     my heart is as thin as the new moon*

*fallen leaves     gathered
for a big fire*

*I was trembling
the turtle invited me into its shell*

*not everyone you meet for the first time
is a stranger*

*the lovers*
*one: I must go*
*other: absence is full of*
*         unheard things*

*one: to other callings*
*other: is that so*

*this sounds like a popular ballad*
*I understand poetry better*

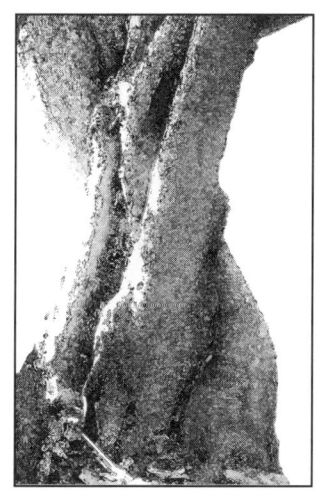

*you hear footsteps in every doorway*  
*but you do not hear the end*  
*you wait in empty spaces*  
*for a final word     that is already*  
*too late*

*and what you understand best*  
*cannot be said*

*evading these dark clouds
a lightbeam danced around
all day long*

*then it rained     and I listened
and I sang my song*

*my respects to the elders*

*also: I may hold you responsible
for allowing me to retain rain*

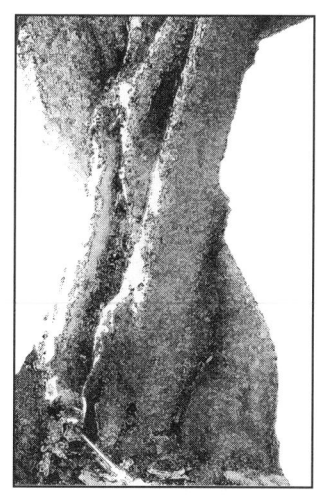

*when this heart was carved in*
*it was springtime*
*my whole being was blooming*
*so it hurt*

*now it is another scar and*
*it still hurts*

*my friend the crow returned*
*holding a red flower*
*scarecrow sneered where did you*
*find this one?   flowers die in the cold*
*the crow knows hothouses     green houses*
*all sorts of houses*

*these stories are told in winter*

*to the story teller:*
*you harvest echoes*
*and through far away voices*
*you fathom mountains*

*somewhere along the way*
*tenderness is lost*

*how could you lose me in a forest*
*I found you in a universe of*
*celestial alleys and ceaseless unrest*

*beloved    I miss you*

*I've missed you ever since the day
sunflowers turned their heads away*

*numbness in chilly nights*
*I shiver and remember*
*ripples on the tiger's skin*
*every season leaves a trail*

*who clarified spring water?*

*full moon*
*my shadows cast a certain sense*
*of foreboding*
*wrap me in snow     wrap me in stars*

*yet another winter is approaching*

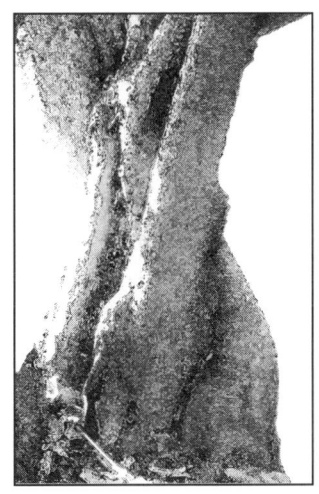

*one had the sparkling eyes of newcomers*
*the other     the voice of a reminiscing flute*
*they were discussing time*
*forever     they said*

*the lovers*

*scarecrow:   you described summer*
*as a shaded walk full of white butterflies*

*I was so concerned for caterpillars*

*today a road reached me*
*I asked where do you go*
*it said I go to the sea and I carry*
*fireflies*
*I asked what do they carry*
*white lies it replied and*
*went away*

*book two*

*this book is dedicated to the absent ones*

*Goli Khalatbary*
*Tehran*
*Autumn 2004*

*Full cycle now—*
*the road has brought hurried travelers*
*and fireflies with their white lies*
*they snowed until my whole being paled*
*in the penance of silence...*
*I asked my friend, the crow*
*what is the penance of silence*
*no-one wears rainbows anymore, was the reply*

*a golden owl was the omen*
*it is time for rain again*

*no settlers yet*
*just passing meteors*
*sowing light dust*
*on severances*

*my heart may be a native*
*of the night sky*
*but I miss so many of you*

*and I miss so much of you*

*the savage treatment wrecked many lives*
*leaving survivors in suspended breath*

*as dawn strings crystal tears*
*pain still howls and moans*
*stirring bruised memories*
*I remember which     I remember why*

*the lovers*
*across the bridge of time*

*one had the restless eyes of nomads*
*the other such a forlorn voice*
*one said: are you still a poet*
*the other: are you yet a dancer*


*in the realm of fairy tales*
*happy ending prevails*

*beloved*

*today*
*my sorrow is so fierce*
*that I could not follow*
*the taming of a wild horse*

*some things have changed*
*I hear bamboos rustling*
*the river exultant on rocks*
*another fall gathering clouds*
*dry leaves     tired footsteps*
*why am I still expectant*

*come and sit by my side*
*if your search is over*
*I'll give you pebbles of hope*
*dreams   love   laughter*

*the sea is not far when*
*the horizon is at high tide*

*scarecrow wears faded colours
my friend the crow custom black
shadows enclose me
in clearly tattered spells*

*I was raised by rain
the sun my playground
wolves my companions
antelopes and wind
my adventures
but when the storm
challenged my roots
it was the dandelions
that held me tight
during the night rages*

*today is luminous*
*I am luminously static*
*stoic   weary    old*

*why is it always cold*

*loving you was like*
*harvesting the sun*

*facing each other*
*an eagle on land*
*and someone kneeling*
*were chatting*
*I had to wonder   was the talk*
*about walking or flying*
*or the garden of rain*
*and its magical fountain*

**the magic depends on the magician's ability to multiply resonances**

*for such a long time now*
*I have reached out for the sky*
*all the birds tease me*
*flying by   soaring high*

*the blue bird to the crow*
*I am blue    why are you black*

*the yellow bird's call*
*sounded like*
*come back come back*

*repetitions*
*confuse*
*constellations*

*if lightening strikes
the roses will be on fire*

*how long till you notice
something is amiss*

*not a single field*
*believes*
*this is the end*
*but I do*

*it has been the end*
*from the beginning*

*butterflies clustered around elders
when the rest of the forest
was supplanted by cinders*

*maybe they will gather
that the rest of the forest
is after all a grave blunder*

*the turtle will tell you
too late is too late*

*strangers become friends
friends turn into strangers*

*which one are you
asked the lovers*

*tenderness has closed shutters*

*the blue planet is turning into red*

*scarecrow's annual farewell:*
*I gift you this season*

*the breeze carries*
*a smell of cold iron*

*will you tie a green thread*
*around a grass blade*
*and pray for renewal*

*the traveler:*
*nostalgia is in my luggage*
*but not regrets*
*there will be other shores*
*other milestones*
*other planets*

*notes:*

*heard the herder hurry*

*saw the serpent slither*

*illusions loiter
the hills are listless*

*nowadays*
*I only laugh with the child*
*most of the others*
*are as intent as hunters*

*to the story teller:*

*use a foreign tongue
to describe beauty
freedom    harmony
alien words may convey
what burnt in my song*

*finally    finally*
*rain fell*
*in a lucid pattern*
*I am no longer beset*
*by the insistent scent*
*of magnolia days*

*my friend the crow asked:*
*what do I do when I'm cornered*
*to do what I don't want to do*

*there are no corners*
*but the ones you devise yourself*

*one had the eyes of loss abrasions*
*the other voiced reconciled visions*
*together they stayed*
*until moonlight swayed*

*the lovers*

*come to think of it
murmured the jasmine
there isn't much difference
between fireflies and fire lies
just enough
to change a lie into a life
and flower gently in mine*

*Born in Tehran, Iran in 1944, Goli Khalatbary followed her father through his diplomatic postings as a girl. She saw many countries, many towns, and many landscapes, but could not have childhood friends. Poetry was the revelation of a summer day in a classroom, at 14, when she glanced at the window and was entranced by the way light transformed a drab scene into one that changed her heartbeat. Her earliest studies were in French, in schools and by correspondence. The full power of art occurred to her like another language when, at 18, she took a course in photography in England. In a career in this field spanning more than 35 years, she produced mostly portraiture and illustrations for poetry.*

*After moving to India she wrote the first book of Diary of a Tree, and showed it as a text exhibition at the India International Center, Delhi.*

*In recent years she has expanded into new media and started working with silver, as well as bronze, iron, stone, and photography. She is now back in Tehran, where she shows her work in yearly exhibitions.*

Copyright © Goli Khalatbari 2006

All rights reserved.
No part of this book may be reproduced
or retransmitted in any manner whatsoever,
except in the form of a review, without the
written permission of the publisher.

library of congress cataloging-in-publication data

Khalatbari, Goli, 1944-
Diary of a tree / Goli Khalatbari.
p. cm.
A poem in two books from the point of view of a tree.
ISBN 1-933823-02-X (pbk. : alk. paper)
I. Title.
PR9507.9.K43D53 2006
821'.92--dc22
2006004308

Printed and Manufactured in the United States

Mage books are available at bookstores,
through the internet
or directly from the publisher:
Mage Publishers, 1032 29th Street, NW, Washington, DC 20007
202-342-1642 • as@mage.com • 800-962-0922
visit Mage online at
www.mage.com